D1716914

V-22 OSPREYS

BY DENNY VON FINN

EPIC

BELLWETHER MEDIA · MINNEAPOLIS, MN

EPIC BOOKS are no ordinary books. They burst with intense action, high-speed heroics, and shadows of the unknown. Are you ready for an Epic adventure?

This edition first published in 2014 by Bellwether Media, Inc.

No part of this publication may be reproduced in whole or in part without written permission of the publisher. For information regarding permission, write to Bellwether Media, Inc., Attention: Permissions Department, 5357 Penn Avenue South, Minneapolis, MN 55419.

Library of Congress Cataloging-in-Publication Data

Von Finn, Denny.
  V-22 Ospreys / by Denny Von Finn.
    pages cm. – (Epic: Military Vehicles)
  Includes bibliographical references and index.
  Summary: "Engaging images accompany information about V-22 Ospreys. The combination of high-interest subject matter and light text is intended for students in grades 2 through 7"– Provided by publisher.
  Audience: Grades 2-7.
  ISBN 978-1-62617-083-4 (hbk. : alk. paper)
  1. V-22 Osprey (Transport plane)–Juvenile literature. 2. Transport planes–United States–Juvenile literature. I. Title.
  UG1242.T7V66 2014
  623.74'65–dc23
                        2013034883

Printed in the United States of America, North Mankato, MN.

The photographs in this book are reproduced through the courtesy of the United States Department of Defense. A special thanks to Ted Carlson/ Fotodynamics for contributing the following photos: front cover, pp. 4-5, 12-13, 20-21.

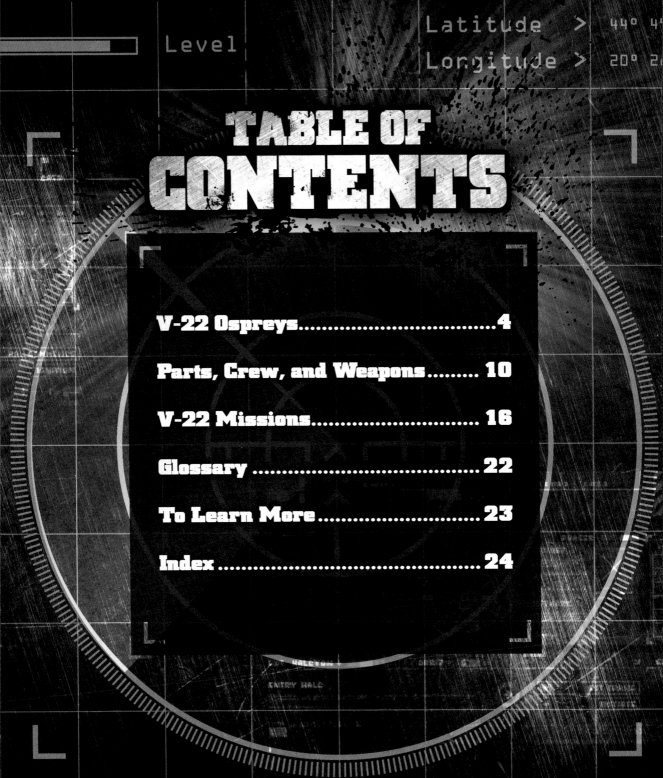

TABLE OF CONTENTS

V-22 OSPREYS

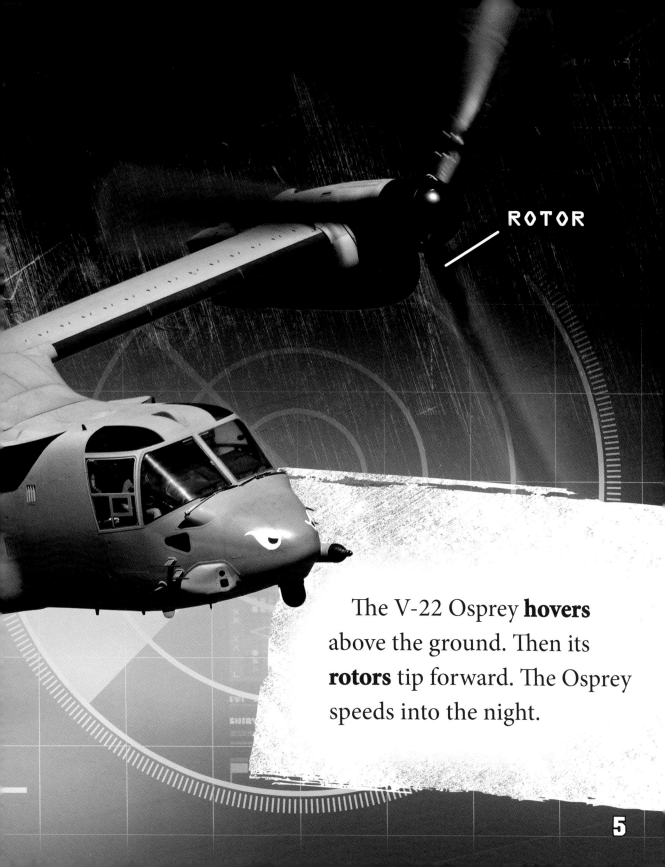

ROTOR

The V-22 Osprey **hovers** above the ground. Then its **rotors** tip forward. The Osprey speeds into the night.

The Osprey races over the desert. It slows as its rotors **tilt** back up. The pilot lands on the rocky ground.

V-22 Osprey Fact

Ospreys used by the U.S. Air Force are called CV-22s. Those used by the Marines are called MV-22s.

The Osprey's back door opens. Marines rush out. The Osprey lifts off. It is gone as quickly as it arrived.

PARTS, CREW, AND WEAPONS

Range |+++++++++++++++++|
0   50   100

Ospreys are military aircraft with special rotors that tilt. They fly like airplanes when their rotors are forward. They tilt their rotors up to take off and land like helicopters.

V-22 Osprey Fact

An Osprey's wings and rotors fold up. This makes it easier to transport.

CARGO AREA

An Osprey's crew sits in the **cockpit**. A large **cargo** area is behind the crew. It can carry 20,000 pounds (9,072 kilograms) of equipment and 24 soldiers.

A V-22 Osprey has 16 fuel tanks. It can also be refueled in flight by another airplane.

COCKPIT

LTCOL E.G. LEBLANC
"BONES"

RESCUE

PUSH BUTTON
PULL HANDLE
OUT 10 FT
WINDOW CUTS
OUT

CARTRIDGE
ACTUATED
DEVICES

Guns protect the Osprey and its crew. A **machine gun** is attached to the bottom of the Osprey. The crew controls it from inside. A soldier can fire another gun from the **cargo ramp**.

MACHINE GUN

CARGO RAMP

V-22 MISSIONS

Ospreys carry **special forces** on dangerous **missions**. They have been used in Iraq and Afghanistan in the **War on Terror**.

MARINES
VMM-265

Ospreys also help people. They rescue pilots who have been shot down. Ospreys have brought food to people in Honduras and Haiti after earthquakes.

Ospreys can take off from aircraft carriers. This helps them make rescue missions at sea.

Ospreys can do all the jobs of a helicopter and an airplane. It is one of the U.S. military's most useful aircraft!

VEHICLE BREAKDOWN:
V-22 OSPREY

Used By:	U.S. Air Force
	U.S. Marine Corps
Entered Service:	2007
Length:	57.3 feet (17.5 meters)
Height:	22 feet (6.7 meters)
Maximum Takeoff Weight:	52,870 pounds (23,981 kilograms)
Wingspan:	84.6 feet (25.8 meters)
Top Speed:	277 miles (445 kilometers) per hour
Range:	575 miles (925 kilometers)
Ceiling:	25,000 feet (7,620 meters)
Crew:	4
Weapon:	one machine gun
Primary Missions:	transport troops, equipment, and supplies; long-range rescue

GLOSSARY

cargo—goods or supplies that a vehicle carries from one place to another

cargo ramp—a sloping platform in the back of an Osprey used to load cargo easily

cockpit—the area of an aircraft where the crew sits

hovers—stays in one place above the ground

machine gun—a weapon that fires bullets rapidly

missions—military tasks

rotors—the spinning parts of an aircraft; Ospreys have two large rotors.

special forces—troops trained to fight in small units with little support

tilt—to tip forward and backward

War on Terror—a war led by the United States to stop organized groups from performing acts of violence; the War on Terror began in 2001.

TO LEARN MORE

At the Library

Alvarez, Carlos. *V-22 Ospreys*. Minneapolis, Minn.: Bellwether Media, 2010.

Hamilton, John. *V-22 Osprey*. Minneapolis, Minn.: ABDO Pub., 2013.

Von Finn, Denny. *Military Helicopters*. Minneapolis, Minn.: Bellwether Media, 2010.

On the Web

Learning more about V-22 Ospreys is as easy as 1, 2, 3.

1. Go to www.factsurfer.com.

2. Enter "V-22 Ospreys" into the search box.

3. Click the "Surf" button and you will see a list of related Web sites.

With factsurfer.com, finding more information is just a click away.

INDEX